Praise for Anne-Marie Verkuijlen

I'm Not Afraid Anymore is a brief, fresh, passionate, and powerful book. Anne-Marie Verkuijlen has moved from survivor to overcomer to skilled professional who helps others on their fierce and essential journey. Readers will both see and feel her heart for victims of oppression. She gives respectful voice to their struggles. More than that, she invites us to respect the nobility of their effort. This book is not light reading—it never intended to be. But it offers major insight and invitation to care. Reading it is an invitation to grow.

— Bill Bagents Professor of Ministry, Counseling, and Biblical Studies
Heritage Christian University

Reading through varied accounts of those fleeing for refuge has helped to bring life to so many who have often become little more than numbers or statistics. In sharing these stories from first-hand experience and a perspective of faith, Anne-Marie Verkuijlen has offered us an insight into the plight of those in genuine need of asylum, whilst also providing a voice to unheard thousands from across the globe. Let me encourage you to join Verkuijlen in her journey with God—a journey of faith, reflection, and self-discovery. It has been a privilege to share in this part of the journey.

— Patrick Boyns Principal, British Bible School

Anne-Marie Verkuijlen invites readers to her counseling experiences with refugees from several nations to Verkuijlen's homeland of the Netherlands. Readers also learn about her personal journey. While respecting counseling ethics and her commitment to confidentiality, Verkuijlen presents stories related to the refugees she worked with during a time of influx of refugees to her country. She gives insight into their fears, challenges, resilience, and hopes. This book challenges readers to learn from these strangers and how helping can change helpers too.

— Rosemary Snodgrass, Ed.D., LPC

I'm Not Afraid Anymore

A Journey into Grace and Understanding

Anne-Marie Verkuijlen

CYPRESS

Copyright © 2025 by Anne-Marie Verkuijlen

Cataloging-in-Publication Data

Verkuijlen, Anne-Marie

I'm not afraid anymore: a journey into grace and understanding / Anne-Marie Verkuijlen.

p. cm.

ISBN: 979-8-89733-005-8 (pbk.); 979-8-89733-006-5 (ebook)

1. Refugees. 2. Refugees—Counseling of. 3. Refugees—Care. 4. Refugees and human rights. 5. Refugees among us. I. Author. II. Title.

616.891408694—dc20

Cover art by Elra Heus- de Graaf (living-arts.nl)

Cover design by Brad McKinnon and Brittany Vander Maas.

All rights reserved.

No part of this book may be reproduced in any form or by any electronic or mechanical means, including information storage and retrieval systems, without written permission from the author, except for the use of brief quotations in a book review.
For information:

Cypress Publications
3625 Helton Drive
PO Box HCU
Florence, AL 35630

www.hcu.edu

This book is dedicated to those who left everything behind to find safety and peace.

And to David and Hannah, whose steadfast faith and courage have profoundly moved me.

Contents

Foreword	xi
Acknowledgments	xv
Preface	xvii
I'm not Afraid Anymore.	1
They Didn't "Just" Leave	7
A Long Road to Safety	13
A Sea of Men: The Silent Stories	19
They Can't "Just" Go Back	25
Mothers: Strength in Struggle	31
Lost Identities	37
In Their Hands: The Weight of Immigration Decisions	43
Life in Emergency Shelters	49
Threads of Connections: Reflections on Working in Emergency Shelters	55
How to Celebrate with Those Who Have Nothing	61
Transformed by Compassion: My Journey Through Refugee Voices	67
From Inspiration to Impact	75
Also by Cypress Publications	77
Heritage Christian University Press	79

Foreword

Through her short book, *I'm Not Afraid Anymore,* Anne-Marie Verkuijlen shares a personal experience that should be inspiring to everyone: Followers of Christ and those who believe in our common humanity, irrespective of national origin, gender, race, or religion. Someone has said, fear has two meanings: **F**orget **E**verything **a**nd **R**un or **F**ace **E**verything **a**nd **R**ise. *I'm Not Afraid Anymore* is an absorbing and inspiring record of how the author decided to face her own fears, only to find unexpected inspiration when God placed her in a work setting where she was asked to help refugees who were also wrestling with their fears.

Although she was not a refugee, Anne-Marie's circumstances allowed her to quickly identify with her clients. Like the refugees, she too had left familiar circumstances and launched out into the fearful unknown. As a woman of faith, Anne-Marie started her new journey with trepidation but was hopeful that God would watch over her. Little did she know that she was following in the footsteps of Peter, who, at the Lord's invitation, had to *put out into the deep and let down his net to take a catch.*

I'm Not Afraid Anymore centers around the riveting but painful stories of the diverse people Anne-Marie encounters during her two-year stint as a counselor to refugees, people of whom she had been critical or at best indifferent. But Anne-Marie does not hesitate to connect the reader to how her challenging work also became a personal journey of growth and renewal that intersected with her personal life. The apostle John wrote, 'perfect love drives out all fear,' and in that spirit, Anne-Marie's journal records her search for a more perfect love. Ultimately, then, *I'm Not Afraid Anymore* is a thoughtful and insightful reflection of values rooted in love that Anne-Marie learned how to intentionally practice.

The stories of the people fleeing to your country or other countries in search of safety will open your eyes and could move you in unexpected ways, just like they heartened Anne-Marie. Expect to be blessed and even transformed because, while opening the eyes of the reader to the plight of refugees, *I'm Not Afraid Anymore* is also a story of personal change. Jesus told Nicodemus that God loves the world, and He also taught that those who give are more blessed than those who receive. Perhaps that is why Paul encouraged the

Galatians to do good to everyone. Even in her fear, Anne-Marie held true to these and other values, and God was able to guide her into uncharted waters where she began to thrive as she poured herself into others. I heartily recommend Anne-Marie's *I'm Not Afraid Anymore*. Join her journey of faith and rejoice in how she healed while helping others navigate their fears as they, too, searched for healing and hope.

Everett Chambers
Charente, France

Everett Chambers, a friend, lawyer, and minister of Christ who encouraged me to write this book.

Acknowledgments

A big thank you to my wonderful sons and daughters-in-law! Your help, support, and encouragement mean so much to me, and I truly appreciate you always being willing to listen to my stories.

To my dear friend and cover designer, Elra Heus, who knows me so well. Thank you for truly understanding this book and capturing its heart so beautifully in your cover design.

I am also grateful to everyone who read early drafts, offered feedback, and helped with editing. Your insights, time, and support strengthened this book, and I'm deeply grateful.

A special thank you to Everett Chambers for encouraging me to write and for writing the foreword. Your belief in me helped give this book its beginning.

Sincere thanks to Bill Bagents, Rosemary Black-Snodgrass, and Patrick Boyns for your generous endorsements. Your reflections have given my book both visibility and validation, I appreciate you lending your voice to this journey.

Deepest gratitude to the Madison Church of Christ for your generous support, which has made a meaningful difference in my life and work. A special thank you to Mike Houts for your guidance and encouragement.

Thank you to HCU for your guidance and commitment in making this book a reality.

A very special thank you to Bill and Laura Bagents.

Bill, thank you for your guidance and support—not only with this book, but above all during the dark moments in my life when I needed it most. I owe where I am today to you.

Laura, thank you for your assistance with my book and for helping me translate some of my thoughts into words.

What makes your help even more profound is that your support was not just for me or this project—it was also a way of honoring the memory of your son, Allen, who was passionate about social justice, kindness, and standing against oppression. With all my heart, thank you.

Preface

When I began working with refugees, I never anticipated the profound impact this endeavor would have on me. I thought I was simply embarking on a mission to assist those in need. But as time went on, I realized that my journey was as much about personal growth as it was about helping others.

I never imagined I would write a book, but sometimes, life takes unexpected turns. My encounters and work with refugees did not happen by chance—through this experience, I've come to see God's hand guiding me in both the process of helping others and in writing this book.

As I shared my experiences, several people encouraged me by telling me, "This needs to be told." And that's what I did. I had so many stories within me, stories I had heard first-hand, that I started simply writing down what I had experienced. The result of that writing is this memoir.

I have gained deep insight from my experiences into the struggles, resilience, and strength of refugees. In writing this book, my goal has been to give them a voice—a voice that has often been unheard or even silenced. I aim to raise awareness about their challenges, share their stories, and highlight their needs.

It is my hope that, from reading these pages, you will not only better understand some of the realities faced by refugees but that you will also be left with a greater appreciation for the power of compassion and connection.

I've had the privilege of working with refugees from over 15 different nations in a variety of settings in the Netherlands. Every refugee shelter is unique, and every staff member works hard to provide care. I acknowledge that my experiences may not be representative of events in all shelters. The experiences I share here come from my time working in these shelters as well as from my personal encounters with refugees.

Disclaimer

Unless otherwise stated, the reader assumes all responsibility for the interpretation and application of the information shared in this book. The author does not accept liability for any actions taken based on the content nor for any harm that may arise from such actions unless otherwise specified. Please be advised that the subject matter discussed in this book may be emotionally intense and sensitive for some readers.

To protect the safety and anonymity of the refugees whose stories are shared in this book, certain details have been altered. Names and other identifying information have been changed or omitted. While some individuals whose stories are included in this book have given explicit permission to share their experiences, others' stories have been blended to reflect the collective refugee experience. While all the quotations included are real and unaltered, they are part of a larger narrative that represents the experiences of many. Any resemblance to real persons is purely coincidental.

I'm not Afraid Anymore.

Unless a grain of wheat falls to the ground and dies, it remains alone; but if it dies, it produces many seeds.

— John 12:24

It was a cold November morning when I chose to walk away from my so-called "certainties" to face an uncertain future. On that day, I packed my personal belongings and left the house I had called my home for over 25 years. The future that stretched before me seemed to hold only darkness, but I feared that remaining where I was held even greater struggle. On that November morning, I felt broken and afraid.

When I closed that door, I had no job. For years, I had spent my time volunteering, serving people in need. However, now I needed a paying job. During the COVID-19 lockdown, the options for finding a job were very limited. I sent out many applications but only received rejections; I was seen either as overqualified or underqualified. Finally, I decided to start my own counselling/coaching practice. I soon found out, however, that the income I gained from this effort was insufficient to meet my basic needs. It seemed as if I was reaching one dead end after another.

My heart has always gone out to people in need and in pain, and despite my own fears and pain, my desire to serve those in pain continued to grow. I began to pray to God, asking for opportunities to serve in this area.

The answer did not come immediately. Nevertheless, I persisted and intensified my request, asking God to lead me to serve where He felt I was needed most. Little did I know that He would answer my prayers in a most unexpected way.

In 2022 war began in Ukraine, with many women and children fleeing their homeland and some coming to my country. These frightened women and children, who had been forced to leave their homes hastily, were in great pain and need. A desire began in my mind and heart to help them. Thanks be to God that in answer to my prayers, I was able to find churches in which He had opened the hearts of the leaders to support me financially so I could dedicate time to be of service to these people.

Yet God was not finished. Because of the experience I was gaining helping refugees, another door also opened for me: I was offered a paying job working in refugee shelters. By accepting this employment, I would be allowing God to focus my passion to help. I was entering a space wherein, by helping others, I would allow Him to continue my own healing and restoration. Finally, it seemed as if God had taken me to the place where He wanted me to be.

It is almost two years since I have begun working with refugees. I provide mental health care and support in various shelters and in a variety of settings. The refugees I work with are from very diverse cultures and of different ages. They range from being highly educated to being illiterate. The common denominator is that they are foreigners in a new country who fled their home country, and are seeking protection.

Prior to becoming involved with refugees, I had

become familiar with images on TV showing the flow of people walking from their homes to different countries in Europe. I had seen videos of boats on the Mediterranean, crowded mostly with men, all on their way to Europe. To be honest, I didn't always know what to think about what I was seeing and, like too many people in destination countries, I thought the flow of people was too great. It seemed like Europe would soon be overrun by refugees and that these people were coming to take our jobs and houses.

I soon began to see shelters where the refugees were housed near me. The news media covered stories of violence breaking out in some of these shelters. These news reports gave me a negative view of the entire group. I also began to see refugees where I lived. Whenever I saw them walking or sitting somewhere, I felt uncomfortable, and my discomfort increased when I encountered male refugees. I especially didn't like it when the men were gathered in groups; I found it quite intimidating.

Now, after almost two years of working intensively with refugees of both sexes, something has changed. I hear their stories; I am aware of what they have gone through and are still going through. I am deeply touched by these stories, by the experiences they have gone through and continue to go through. They were all fearful for their lives and had embarked on a journey in search of safety for themselves and for their families.

My heart has been touched: I see their faces, I appreciate their tears, I share their sorrow, and I feel their pain. But I also see their unshed tears. Tears that they cannot yet allow to flow lest they become an uncontrollable floodgate. I see real faces; I now see them as human. I also see that there are parallels between their story and my story, between their journey and my journey.

I'm not afraid anymore.

They Didn't "Just" Leave

Then he summoned Moses and Aaron by night and said, "Up, go out from among my people, both you and the people of Israel; and go, serve the LORD, as you have said. Take your flocks and your herds, as you have said, and be gone, and bless me also!"

— Exodus 12:31–32

Many people freely choose to leave their country for a variety of reasons, often in the hope of a better life elsewhere. Under "normal" circumstances, they can decide at any time whether or not to return to their home country. It is definitely not the same for the people with whom I work. Refugees are people who have been forced to flee their home countries due to war, violence, or persecution due to their religion, political beliefs, sexual preference, or even because they are members of a specific ethnic group. They cannot return home until conditions in their country of origin are safe. No one knows when, or if, that will occur.

In many cases, they have had to flee suddenly and without warning or time to prepare for their departure. They often do not have time to think before they have to act. There is not much time to pack a suitcase. Besides that, how much can you take with you if you have to make your flight by foot? How much luggage are you able to carry? Sometimes, there isn't even time for refugees to say goodbye to anyone. Sometimes it's too dangerous to say goodbye. That was the case for Anan.

Anan had a wife and two girls aged 12 and 15. They lived in a small village in a house with a little garden. The family had two cats that the younger girl especially loved. Anan had a good job with many responsibilities. He was very dedicated to his job, a job that he enjoyed very much.

His life changed dramatically when, after the coup in his home country, he was declared a terrorist (just like many others) and removed from his position. He was in jail for two years before being released, but another prison sentence awaited him. During his first imprisonment, he had to share a 20 square meter (215 square foot) cell with 20 other people. He made the very difficult decision to flee the country to avoid more years in prison.

Anan arranged his flight in secret. It was too risky for him to inform his children or even his wife about his plans. If his children accidentally said something to others, it would mean that he would immediately be arrested by the police, imprisoned, tortured, or perhaps killed. Anan knew when the time had come that he should say goodbye to his family, but he had to remain silent for his safety. How difficult that must have been!

His family didn't know anything at the time, but they found out a day later that he had fled the country. They had not been able to say goodbye to their husband and father. This was, of course, very hard for his family and for him. He knew he wouldn't be able to see them for a while. His younger daughter especially missed him very much. Anan showed me a message from her, a big heart with the text: "When will I see you again, daddy? I miss you so much!" He had tears in his eyes.

Even while trying to find his way, Anan faced new struggles. People from his home country became aware of his circumstances, mistreating him and labelling him a traitor.

Anan asked for my help in facing his new reality while simultaneously managing his past. It was very difficult, after having served your country for many years, to be seen as a traitor. Anan was a decent, strong, and honest man who had men serving under him. A man who was determined to work hard. At our final meeting, he said, "I promise you I will do my utmost for this country once I get a residence permit." I still see this man of integrity sitting on his chair, and I was touched by the deep love with which he spoke about his family.

Unlike Anan, when God decided to get Israel out of Egypt (Exodus 12), His people wanted to leave. They were able to pack their belongings and bring their families with them. Anan was able to pack a suitcase, but didn't want to leave. For others, there was no time even to pack their things. Some had to flee in such a hurry that they only had the clothes they were wearing.

I see people whose country of birth can no longer be their home. People who had not much or nothing to choose. Sometimes their reality is to die or to flee. These people come to "our" country, having given up everything. They have left everything they are familiar with and the people they love. They have left behind everything that is near and dear to them.

And here they are in a foreign country, "our" country, a completely different country for them, with all the emotional baggage that they carry with them. What a world! This is their world, and this is their reality. Most are not looking for a better life, but they are looking for protection, security, and peace.

They didn't "just" leave.

A Long Road to Safety

And Moses said to the people, "Fear not, stand firm, and see the salvation of the LORD, which he will work for you today. For the Egyptians whom you see today, you shall never see again. The LORD will fight for you, and you have only to be silent."

— Exodus 14:13–14

OF THE PEOPLE who must flee their country, only a few can simply get in a car or take the train or plane. They often need a visa to leave their country—visa that is only granted under certain strict conditions. Without a visa, it is not possible for refugees to travel by plane or ferry, as these companies are required to refuse people without a visa. Refugees who cannot cross a border legally need help, and that help they buy from a smuggler.

Unlike the Israelites, who were guided and protected by God during the Exodus, refugees find themselves at the mercy of strangers. And those strangers often show no mercy.

The route many take to reach Europe is via the Mediterranean Sea and with the help of a smuggler. While smugglers do help refugees to leave their countries, the crossings are very costly and often extremely dangerous. In the eyes of a smuggler, a human life does not count.

Ali was one of those who took the route via the Mediterranean Sea. His wife and his little baby stayed behind in his home country with the intention of travelling to Europe later. Ali's flight took him through Libya, where he spent 3.5 years, longer than he had thought and hoped. During his first attempt to cross by boat to Italy, he fell out of the boat and ended up in the water. The Libyan coast guard intercepted him and forcibly returned him to Libya, where he was detained for two years.

Refugees intercepted while crossing the Mediterranean Sea end up in Libyan detention centers, where they are forced to perform labor; they are tortured, extorted, and, in the worst cases, murdered. Ali eventually managed to reach Europe, but he tells me that after his time in Libyan prison and the horrors he witnessed and experienced there, he feels like he has no future. During our first meeting, Ali gave me this brief outline of his journey to safety, seemingly without showing emotions. However, I could see the tears he could not shed behind his eyes. What an enormous amount of suffering, pain, and sorrow lies behind his story!

Others make their journey entirely on foot. No cars, trains, or buses for them- they only have their shoes. A few years ago, I saw images on TV of people making their way to safer places. I saw large numbers of people on foot, long lines of people that seemed to stretch endlessly.

One of them was Jamal. He is from a country where, due to circumstances of violence, he had to flee. This young man, about 20 years old, came to Europe on foot, which means he walked about 4,300 miles. His journey took him eight months to complete, eventually reaching my country. Along the way, in the neighbouring countries, he was able to stay with fellow countrymen who had left his country earlier and who provided him with food. I hope they gave Jamal some extra care, given his young age and the fact that he was travelling alone. When crossing national borders, he was sent back by the police several times. In Europe, he stayed in refugee camps before finally arriving in my country.

He left his parents and sister behind in his home country and fled to escape the severe violence he had to endure in his country. His father was arrested by a fundamentalist group and is in prison. Jamal does not know anything about how his father is doing. He does not know if his father is even alive.

Contact is not possible, and Jamal is very uncertain about his father's fate. I try to imagine covering about 4,300 miles on foot, walking for eight months, and not always on decent roads. I try to picture what it would be like to walk that distance. How much luggage would I be able to carry, pops up in my mind. As a mother, I try to imagine my children undertaking such a journey so that I would have to say goodbye to them and not know where they might end up. Many mothers have had to say goodbye to their sons in this way, and they don't know if they'll ever see their children again.

This is Jamal, a friendly young man who could be my son in terms of age. His dream is to become a tailor. He doesn't speak English, so we communicate via a translation app. A sweet young man whose response to my announcement of a two-week leave was mistranslated by the translation app as "I will not miss you." That put a big smile on my face. A friendly boy like him would never say that, and I know that translation apps don't always translate correctly! Paying close attention is always a first requirement. It gives us an opportunity to laugh, which is also important. One day, the manager said to me, "Jamal looks so happy now; he must be in love." Better than falling in love, he had been able to speak to his mother and sister, with whom he had had no contact for ten months.

Ali and Jamal were only two of the many on their way to a safer place. Two of the faceless people in boats on the Mediterranean Sea, and the huge stream of people walking that I saw on TV. It is different now; I know stories of people among them. I no longer see throngs from a distance. I see people, each with his or her unique personality and feelings.

It is bizarre that I have always had a heart for people in need, but at that time, I did not consider this group of people as people in need.

A Sea of Men: The Silent Stories

Now the LORD said to Abram, "Go from your country and your kindred and your father's house to the land that I will show you.

— *Genesis* 12:1

It always struck me that I saw so many men when I saw images of refugees on TV, men who often sat in groups at the reception center or downtown. The majority of residents at the shelters are also men. Now and then, I saw men with their families or partners, but they usually came alone. Many have left their families behind in their home country. I had mixed feelings about that, and I wasn't the only one who had them. I wondered how it was possible that these men would leave their wives and children behind in a country where there is war, violence, and persecution. I learned two important lessons about this from conversations with these groups of men, lessons that changed my attitude.

The amounts paid to leave a country using a smuggler are very high. From a few thousand euros up to 15,000-20,000 euros per person. That is already a lot for one person, let alone a family of four or more. For many, it is unaffordable. In addition, the journey is both dangerous and exhausting. Those factors make many men flee the country without their families and apply for asylum in Europe. When they receive a residence permit, they can bring their family over based on family reunification laws, depending on the country where they end up. In reunification circumstances, women and children can obtain a visa for travel out of their country. It is a journey that is still not without risks for everyone, but it is legal.

Many of these men are married and have children,

like Youssef. Youssef was married and had three children, ages one, four, and eight. He feared for his life and quickly left his home country, leaving his wife and children behind. His wife was pregnant at the time, and his youngest son was born four months after he left. Youssef thus became a father, yet one who had only been able to see his child in photos and via video calling. He had never been able to hold his baby son in his arms. How difficult it was for a new father, and it was hard for the rest of the family as well! In fact, Youssef's youngest son was a child who officially didn't exist in his home country because Youssef, as the father, had not been able to register the birth of his new son.

Youssef had a very special bond with his daughter. His little girl, who was four years old, was too young to understand what had happened, so she couldn't understand why her father had left. With his voice full of emotion, Youssef told me that his daughter regularly told him that he had abandoned her. He knew she was too young to understand why he had to leave the country, but that didn't make the words of such a small child any less painful. As a father, he wanted to be there for his family and provide for them, but that was not possible for him. How much love, pain, and longing underlie his quiet, simple statement: "I smile now, but my soul cries."!

Most fathers asked me whether I had children of my own. After confirming, I always noticed a subtle change in their attitude towards me. They became more open and less afraid of making themselves vulnerable. Perhaps the fact that I am a mother gave them the knowledge that I, as a parent, could empathize with their situation at least in part.

These fathers love their children dearly, and I have seen many of their family pictures. They proudly show me photos of their children, often with tears in their eyes. They also know that their families are in difficult circumstances. It is because of these circumstances that they fled and had to make the terrible decision to leave their families behind.

At one of the shelters where I worked, I met Samuel. Before he became my client, I knew him by sight as he walked around the shelter. I saw him do nothing but look at me and others with an angry look in his eyes. Only after I spoke to him personally during one of our sessions did I learn about his background.

Samuel was a man who had experienced a lot in his home country and during his flight. He told me that he had been forced to serve in the army of an oppressive regime for a long time, in an army where he was always trained to show this angry facial expression. If someone has been forced, trained, and taught for years to have a facial expression like this, that doesn't change overnight. Certainly not if life has given you few or no reasons to smile.

Youssef and Samuel were only two men from a sea of men. They were utterly unlike Abram in Genesis 12 and following. They were leaving their homelands to preserve their lives. They did not leave based on a call from God or because of a promise from God of a blessed future. Rather than leaving in hope, they were leaving out of desperation and fear.

Before I started this job, I really had no idea why I saw so many men. I found them very intimidating, including Samuel, the man who stared at me with an angry look. Now I know that many of them had to make choices that a person should never have to make. How urgent must their need be for them to make such a decision? Many men are alone in Europe, and only now do I realize that it is not so strange that they are grouping. It is lonely in a foreign country, and they also need company and support. They find that with each other. What else could I expect from them at a time when they can do little else and are allowed to do little else than wait for an answer to their asylum application?

They Can't "Just" Go Back

And they sat with him on the ground seven days and seven nights, and no one spoke a word to him, for they saw that his suffering was very great.

—*Job* 2:13

IF YOU HAVE FLED your country, you cannot simply return home. That statement seems very contradictory on a basic level, namely, why would you want to go back if you have fled?

Refugees leave their country for a variety of reasons. But everyone who flees leaves behind family and friends in their home country, people who are dear to them. Often, the refugees are men who undertake the journey to Europe and, later, after obtaining a residence permit, bring their wives and children safely over in the context of family reunification.

I had never realized that until I spoke to Araz, one of my first clients, a Kurd. For decades, Kurds in his home country have been the victims of constant attacks on their ethnic, cultural, religious identity, and economic and political status by successive governments. Araz could no longer visit his home country due to the significant risk of arrest. He couldn't go back in case of illness or the death of a family member. Would he ever be able to see and hug his loved ones again? "Sometimes, I am overwhelmed by the desire to return home, and sometimes have thoughts about that," Araz told me once. It wasn't easy, although he tried to make the best of his circumstances.

In February 2023, a major earthquake struck Turkey and Syria, killing more than 55,000 people and leaving millions homeless. Among the refugees in Europe are many men whose wives and children were still in those earthquake-affected areas. The media showed many images of the earthquake, with the devastation and the crying people. For me, the images became living people—people with faces and emotions, people with family who lived in the earthquake area, family members whose homes were severely damaged, family members who died or were seriously injured. I saw men with huge concerns and fear for their wives and children. Their children were traumatized after the earthquake. Their wives were desperate because there was no money, they were in financial difficulties, and they had terrible living conditions. The stress of these men was intense; they couldn't protect their families, and their desperation was great.

While Araz couldn't return home due to well-founded fear, Moussa grappled with the hardships his family faced in the aftermath of the earthquake. Moussa was a friendly and quiet man who had already been in my country for a while before I met him. He was married, and his wife and two children were still in his home country. He missed his family very much, but he stayed strong, and it was doable for him. However, the earthquake changed everything. In situations where the man flees, it is often the parents who help the wife and children. Unfortunately for Moussa's wife, there were no parents left alive to support his family. After their house was destroyed, his wife lived with their children in a tent. After the heavy earthquake, there were many aftershocks. Their youngest son, who was nine years old, was terrified; he didn't dare to go to sleep. Moussa told me that during conversations with his family, his son cried on the phone because he was so scared. He asked his father to come and get him.

"How much can someone endure?" Moussa asked me. He and many other fathers were desperate because their families were in dire need, and they, as husbands and fathers, could do literally nothing to help them. They begged me, if it was possible, to speed up the application process and have their families come over. Unfortunately, with the multitude of rules and procedures, there was absolutely no possibility. And traveling to the country they'd fled would create significant negative consequences for their asylum status.

My job was to support these desperate men in their grief. In such distressing situations, there are actually almost no words that are helpful, and silence is often more powerful and comforting for these fathers. This silence is also reflected in Job 2:13, where his friends sat with Job on the ground for seven days and seven nights, and no one spoke a word to him, for they saw that his suffering was very great. Silence can express empathy, understanding, and respect. It can also show that you are genuinely listening and trying to understand. Silence, along with the universal prayer sign, gave these fathers some comfort.

Because Moussa had sought psychological help and I was aware of his psychological state, I was able to do something for him on a small scale. He could be transferred to a shelter in an area where he had friends living. Friends who could give him the support he so badly needed. Support from family and/or friends is essential in difficult times. Asking for help is not always easy and can have a considerably high threshold, especially if one comes from a culture in which accepting—or even seeking—psychological help is seen as a weakness. Fortunately, I could do this for Moussa because he had sought my help.

People who flee a country for extraordinary reasons know they can't "just" go back home. However, knowing that his family lives in challenging conditions can make a man yearn to return. What a situation like this does to a person is indescribable. I do not have words suitable or adequate for sharing all I have heard, but let me try.

Put yourself in the skin of one of these men. Imagine having to flee in order to save your life—leaving your entire family and all of your friends behind in your home country. And then imagine hearing that your loved ones are facing hunger, poverty, mistreatment, and other dire circumstances. Imagine hearing your young children begging you to come back home because they are so scared. Imagine being told that a loved one is seriously ill or has died. What do you do? What CAN you do? How many options do you have? Do you have ANY options? That is why people who can never return home would ever consider going back!

Mothers: Strength in Struggle

Strength and dignity are her clothing, and she laughs at the time to come. She opens her mouth with wisdom, and the teaching of kindness is on her tongue. She looks well to the ways of her household and does not eat the bread of idleness. Her children rise up and call her blessed.

— *Proverbs 31:25–28*

Most people at the shelters where I work travel alone. A minority of them are couples, some with children. Sometimes, I see single mothers with their children; these women have fled their home country seeking protection for their children and themselves in Europe. However, for many, finding safety and relief when reaching Europe was not the case. Several refugees told me stories about the harsh conditions they encountered in camps along the Balkan route, including inferior hygiene, lack of sleep, and insufficient food and water. They also reported violence and abuse. Women and children are especially vulnerable. This is often the reality of female refugees, and even more so for those with children. Fleeing as a mother with your children, imagine!

At one of the shelters, I met one of those single mothers, Leyla. A cheerful and bright woman in her late thirties, she always waved at me and greeted me with a big smile when she saw me at the shelter. After a certain time, she made an appointment with me. That began a series of many sessions that lasted until the shelter closed its doors and Leyla and her children were transferred to another part of the country.

Leyla, a mother of two, had to leave her home country with her children due to government actions related to her beliefs. Their journey took them through the Balkans, mostly on foot. Her daughter was still very young and had to be carried for much of the journey. It was a blessing that Leyla's son could help her carry the little girl. In her home country, she had already experienced lots of hardship. There were, again, many trials and difficulties in the Balkans during their journey to my country. There was hunger, thirst, fatigue, and the risk of getting injured—and there was violence. "Here, I saw people without conscience and no moral sense; there were moments when I thought that I and my children would die," Leyla said. I learned that lady, with her beautiful smile, had gone through a lot of pain. However, she couldn't afford a breakdown. She had to remain strong for the children for whom she was responsible.

Her little girl saw many horrible situations on her way to my country and needed the constant presence of her mother to feel safe. Her son was in his teenage years. Besides the physical and emotional changes that come with growing up, he also had to deal with the fact that his life had changed radically. Yet he remained a teenager with behavior that is typical for teenagers. One day, with a touch of irony, his mother said about him: "He is training his throwing skills by tossing his shirt in the laundry basket so that he doesn't have to get up from his bed and can just stay there."

Leyla found it very comforting to have a safe place with me to process what had happened, reset her emotions, and allow herself to cry. "I always have to be strong as a mother. I have never been able to cry so comfortably. It gives me relief from the feeling of being 70 years old," were her words during a session when she was exhausted. Leyla needed a place where she didn't have to be strong and could just be herself, however she felt, free to unload, breathe, receive, and to be Leyla. Just because people are strong doesn't mean they can't ask for help or that they don't need help. Seeking help helped Leyla stay strong. I felt honored to walk alongside her during the time we had.

As a parent, you want to provide your children with a stable home, but circumstances in your home country may make it impossible for you to offer your children the gift of consistency. It is quite a decision to pick up your children and take them away from everything familiar to them.

Despite all she has been through, Leyla was not a victim. She was very active in initiating creative activities at the shelter and in caring for other families' little ones. One day, she beamed and told me she had been allowed to cook—to prepare a meal for her children and herself—to feed them food that she knew they would enjoy. I was so pleased to see the sparkle in her eyes.

Then came the day of our final meeting. Our farewell occurred because Leyla and her children were transferred to another shelter. She shared that she had heard that her mother was terminally ill. Tears rolled down her cheeks as she expressed her deep desire to be with her, but that was impossible. How very, very sorry I felt for her to hear this. And this was our last meeting!

She hugged me as if she knew it would be the last

time she saw me. She hugged me as if she knew she was leaving her safe place and that she had to be strong, alone, again.

Beautiful, brave Leyla, may you have people around you at your new place with whom you feel safe and welcome so that you can remain a stable factor for your children!

Lost Identities

She said to them, "Do not call me Naomi; call me Mara, for the Almighty has dealt very bitterly with me. I went away full, and the LORD has brought me back empty. Why call me Naomi, when the LORD has testified against me and the Almighty has brought calamity upon me?"

— *Ruth* 1:20–21

THE REFUGEES STAYING at the shelters come from different layers of society. While many have few, if any, possessions, some individuals previously enjoyed what they describe as "a good life" in their home countries. Some had good jobs, warm and close family ties, and strong friendships. Several earned a substantial income and were respected by many. They had no desire to leave until circumstances forced them to flee.

One of the people who expressed having had a good life in her home country was Ayda. For herself at that time, there was no direct danger, but for her husband there was. Her husband was risking imprisonment because of his political beliefs. When he was preparing to leave the country, she made the decision to join him and to take along their 8-year-old daughter. The reason she told me she did this was her desire to keep the family intact and to make sure that her daughter would have her father with her. For many, however, bringing the family is not possible, and this adds to the sadness of being separated from one another for a long time.

While Ayda was able to keep her family together, her life changed dramatically. She was uprooted, and everything she once held onto was gone. In a short time, her various roles had been drastically reduced. Her daily routines had disappeared, and her social life had been completely disrupted. In this new country, she struggled with the question: Who am I now? No one here knew her unique qualities and skills or what she had achieved in her life. Many viewed her only as a "refugee" or "foreigner." But "refugee" and "foreigner" are not identities. This loss of familiar roles, a sense of community, and a lack of recognition deeply affected her self-esteem.

The book of Ruth tells about Naomi, whose husband and two sons died. Naomi felt that she had been robbed of her identity; because of the depth of her grief, she changed her name to Mara, which means "bitter." Her self-image was defined by the grief she faced. Naomi found her identity in being a wife and mother. With the loss of her husband and children, she now finds identity in their absence, in the emptiness and bitterness of her life. Her story shows the profound impact of losing familiar roles. Similar to her, all refugees struggle with the loss of identities and roles.

The lack of recognition as an individual is a painful experience for many. As a young man in his 20s told me during a conversation, he often felt reduced to a number. He was visibly emotional when he answered my question about his education. "Since I left my country, you are the first to ask me about my education. You treat me like a human being," he said. His emotional reaction once again impressed upon me the importance of seeing people as individuals. The refugee label, together with the dismissive attitude that some people hold towards refugees, doesn't make it easier for them. Some feel rejected by their own country and government—and also unwelcome in this country. They, too, follow the media reports. The often traumatic journey and the experiences they have gone through can affect refugees' self-image and confidence, which in turn affects their personal identity. In addition, they have lost their familiar environment and roles. The world with which they are familiar has completely fallen apart.

One of the people who also struggled with this was Natalya. She was a single mother who was proud of her two young adult daughters studying abroad. In her home country, she had a good life. She worked as a teacher in an elementary school with passion and joy. Her family lived nearby and she had a close circle of friends. She enjoyed life to the fullest. Then the war broke out, and because she lived in the center of the war zone, she was forced to flee. Now she found herself in a country where she had never been before.

All her friends had also fled and had ended up scattered across different countries worldwide. Her entire social network was gone, and she had the status of a refugee. "Here I am nothing," she told me, reflecting the words of many others. She longed to return to her homeland, but the circumstances were too dangerous. Even if she could, her country would never be the same again, even when the war ends. She was very aware of that. She mourned for her country, which would never be the country she once knew.

What had been very helpful to her in coping with her situation was that she had started to commit herself to her fellow countrymen here. Along with another lady, she organized craft gatherings. Though she didn't consider herself very talented, this gave her a sense of purpose. At the same time, she brought women together, and they shared their worries and sorrows. For Natalya, it was a completely new experience; it did her good, and I was happy to see her blossom. What a beautiful initiative of hers!

For those still awaiting a decision on their residence status, their identity remains linked to the label "refugee." For them, daily life is a struggle filled with uncertainty. In contrast, refugees who are granted residence permits embark on a journey of rebuilding their lives and forming a new identity. Who are you now that the roles you previously had have changed? Who are you going to be? This will be a process of regrowth in new territory.

Identity is a dynamic process for refugees, a continuous search for meaning connected with the challenges and hope in their lives. Their story is one of loss and resilience, and for those who are granted a residence permit, it is also one of rebuilding. It is a process through which they relearn who they are in the midst of the change that has befallen them.

In Their Hands: The Weight of Immigration Decisions

Therefore, since we are surrounded by so great a cloud of witnesses, let us also lay aside every weight, and sin which clings so closely, and let us run with endurance the race that is set before us, looking to Jesus, the founder and perfecter of our faith, who for the joy that was set before him endured the cross, despising the shame, and is seated at the right hand of the throne of God.

— Hebrews 12:1–2

ALL REFUGEES ARRIVING in my country must register as asylum seekers with the Immigration and Naturalization Service (to which I will refer as simply immigration from now on). This is the beginning of their asylum procedure. Every asylum seeker has to undergo interviews with immigration. Some individuals register as refugees but come to this country for reasons other than safety. Therefore, it is crucial to consider carefully each person's background and circumstances. Especially for those who are facing persecution, the interviews with immigration can be very stressful. They worry about whether the immigration officials will believe their story. Another significant source of stress is the need for an interpreter during these interviews. There is a risk of miscommunication, and asylum seekers feel uncertain about whether their answers will be accurately translated.

The law states that the immigration service has six months to decide on an asylum application. However, due to a backlog due to the high number of asylum applications compared with the number of decisions made and because of the increase in family reunifications, this period has been extended to 15 months. It was more the rule than the exception that this period was itself exceeded.

During the time I've worked at these shelters, I've observed that the waiting time for asylum seekers from countries at war was generally shorter compared with those seeking asylum for other, more strictly personal

In Their Hands: The Weight of Immigration Decisio... 45

reasons. I have met individuals who have been waiting for a decision from immigration for more than two years. All this time, they have remained uncertain about their future and their fate.

Their fates and futures are entirely in the hands of immigration. A six-month wait for an immigration decision is already a long time for anyone who has fled their country, let alone waiting for a year or even longer. They do not know whether their future will be in this country, and if it is not, what will happen to them then? The waiting is almost unbearable for those who know their lives are in great danger if they are forced to return home.

Sometimes, refugees would ask me what I thought the immigration decision would be, but I could not and should not answer that question. I could consider this by myself and decide that what person A or B had experienced were valid grounds for a residence permit, but I couldn't share these thoughts with anyone. As much as I would have liked to express something positive about the outcomes, I could not. While hope is essential, it's vital to avoid raising false expectations, especially when it comes to individuals in these circumstances. This means a very tense time for everyone. For those who have reasonable grounds to fear for their lives if they are sent back to their home country, the decision of the immigration service is a matter of life and death.

A poignant example of this is the story of Elias, a

young man who was here all alone. He was immensely grateful for his place in the shelter and for the extra clothing he had received. This young man in his early twenties was mature, well-spoken, and very intelligent. He connected easily with others and shared his faith whenever he could. While waiting for the answer from immigration, he was helpful to the staff at the shelter, was active in volunteer work, and even managed to get a paid job after a while. The staff at the shelter were very happy with him; I often heard them say that Elias was always so kind and helpful, always having an eye out for the well-being of others.

Elias escaped from his home country because of persecution of his faith. He knew if he was ever sent back to his home country, that a certain group of men would track him down and that he would not survive. The thought of his application being rejected caused him great anxiety about what would happen to him next. I saw the fear in his eyes, and there was nothing I could do to take away that fear, no matter how much I wished I could. I could try to empathize with his situation, but it was impossible to truly know and understand what it felt like for him. While he was safe in this country, there was a significant difference between being safe and feeling secure. He once confided in me that it felt like being "someone who can't swim and is left in the middle of the sea." It is too easy to suggest to someone anxious about the outcome, "Let it go," or say things like "Try not to think about it all the time." It is nearly impossible not to think and worry about the outcome of the asylum procedure, especially at night when one lies awake for hours. Everything seems worse at night. The uncertainty and fear can be overwhelming and significantly impact one's sleep and physical and mental condition. For Elias, this meant dealing with the unknown while trying to cope with the fear and stress as best as he could.

In Hebrews 11, at the end of listing several men and women and their faith, the Bible talks about those who, although they waited and went through times of severe suffering, their names may never be known. Their stories may never be heard, but they still had to go through these things. What was significant about them, though, was their faith. They waited through faith. We are called to look at their suffering and see the faith that they showed through their suffering and waiting as an example for us all. Hebrews 12 introduces the next chapter by saying that these "refugees" are our example and witness. Through the trials, we look to Jesus, who perfected our faith, making it possible for us to fall short, to sit in uncertainty, to experience emotional turmoil, and yet still be redeemed.

Sometimes all I could do was be present, walking alongside Elias as he took each step forward. This whole situation was incredibly difficult, but he stayed firm in his faith. It takes a lot of strength not to be filled with fear while waiting. I have a deep respect for those who have valid grounds to fear for their lives when returning to their home country but are doing all they can to keep on going and moving while waiting in uncertainty and holding on tightly to God. In the waiting, it's important to rely on God for strength and to let Him work. What an example Elias set for me and for others around him! It was an honor to walk with him on his path and a real blessing to get to know this young man called Elias.

(Dear Reader, I know this topic may be heavy and dark. In order to have compassion for these people, you as a reader must know their reality. I believe it's important to understand this reality so we can truly empathize with others. Compassion comes from knowing the whole story!)

Life in Emergency Shelters

As soon as he had finished speaking to Saul, the soul of Jonathan was knit to the soul of David, and Jonathan loved him as his own soul. And Saul took him that day and would not let him return to his father's house. Then Jonathan made a covenant with David, because he loved him as his own soul.

— *1 Samuel* 18:1–3

As a refugee, you end up at an asylum-seeking center in my country. This could be an asylum seekers' center where individuals could prepare food, participate in activities, and start learning the language. Due to a shortage of these centers for a number of years, emergency shelters had been set up. At these shelters, people received basic necessities like a bed, bathroom access, and food. Initially, these shelters were intended for a maximum stay of three days. However, while working at these emergency shelters, I met people who had been staying there for more than a year. Families shared one small unit, and single travellers shared a unit with others. They used communal showers and toilets. These shelters were all built to be temporary, sometimes set up for just a few months, meaning that everyone was supposed to be transferred to another shelter when one closed. Some refugees, however, had stayed in more than four shelters within a year. "The most difficult part of this process is that you build up a little bit, and then you have to start over again," said those who had experienced multiple transfers.

In addition to the challenges of living arrangements, another significant issue within these shelters was the restriction on cooking, which wasn't allowed in the units. Instead, meals were served three times a day in a communal area. Occasionally, media reports highlighted refugees protesting the food quality, which irritated many in my country who believed they should be grateful for getting any food at all. At one of the shelters, a catering provider kindly served me a hot meal after work, sparing me a long drive home on an empty stomach. While I appreciated the food, I realized I wouldn't be happy either if I got only this bulk food. This made me understand them better. In addition, most people have little to nothing to do during the day, and the moments when they eat are the day's highlight.

Depending on the shelters' size and location, people could participate in some activities such as language learning and painting lessons, but on a much smaller scale than in the official asylum-seeking centers. In my country, refugees are not allowed to work for the first six months after arrival. They are allowed to do volunteer work, but that also depends on the efforts and capabilities of each shelter to help them with that. After six months, they are allowed to work under certain conditions. Not many can do so because of language barriers or the traumas they have experienced. In addition, they are faced with bureaucratic procedures that can discourage them.

Due to a lack of work and other activities, many had a lot of time to think and worry. They were concerned about family in their home country, and there was uncertainty about whether or not they would be allowed to stay in this country. They also didn't know how long it would take before the interviews regarding their asylum applications would take place. The best remedy for this would be distraction and keeping busy. However, this wasn't easy for them at these shelters with minimal activities. What they could do was spend time outdoors and exercise, which would work positively for them. Some started exercising enthusiastically and were very determined to do so every day. However, if you have all the time in the world to walk outside day after day, that is completely different.

One such individual navigating these challenges was Yasmin. Yasmin was a young woman of 20 who had a good education but unfortunately couldn't finish it due to circumstances in her home country. Her mother had passed away and her father and three sisters were still in her home country. They were in no position to flee. Yasmin was an intelligent young lady who knew how to tackle things and enthusiastically threw herself into learning the language. She had made a weekly schedule with cycling routes to keep exercising and staying fit. She independently went looking for volunteer work and later a paid job. However, the shelter where she stayed was situated in a region where the possibilities for her were very limited, and Yasmin wasn't able to work, paid or unpaid. In addition, she had to wait a long time for her immigration interview, whereas others didn't. Slowly, I saw her change from an optimistic woman into a woman who struggled more and more. "I am starting to lose hope," she once told me. The uncertainty and worry were taking a toll on her mental health, but she worked very hard to stay healthy mentally as well as physically.

While staying in these shelters, the support of friends and family can offer a lifeline. Every now and then, Yasmin visited friends in another part of the country. They were a family with children her age. She liked to feel that she had a home for a weekend now and then, where she could enjoy some parental care from people the same age as her parents. It is a great advantage if refugees have family or friends nearby. For Yasmin, her visits to friends in another part of the country provided a much-needed respite from her daily struggles.

This kind of support resembles the friendship between David and Jonathan, as described in 1 Samuel 18–20, a beautiful example of encouragement and support during difficult times. Jonathan consistently stood by David in his darkest moments. Their relationship highlights the importance of communal support, which gives strength and hope, especially to those facing adversity. The relationship between Jonathan and David also demonstrates the importance and value of building and sustaining a community that can lift up individuals going through tough times, similar to the vital emotional support provided to Yasmin by her friends. I am glad that Yasmin had them, but some refugees have no access to friends or family. Compassionate strangers can—and should—step forward to help fill their needs.

When I finished working at her shelter, she thanked me with the words, "Thank you for listening to my complaining." I clarified to her that I would not label her words as complaining but rather as venting her emotions. They helped her process her thoughts and emotions during these challenging circumstances in her life. This young lady showed determination and resilience despite the constraints of her environment. Amidst uncertainty, Yasmin's ability to adapt and seek support gave her hope.

Threads of Connections: Reflections on Working in Emergency Shelters

Two are better than one, because they have a good reward for their toil. For if they fall, one will lift up his fellow. But woe to him who is alone when he falls and has not another to lift him up!

— *Ecclesiastes 4:9–10*

STEPPING into this job as a psychologist in emergency shelters was a unique and challenging opportunity for me. All shelters were quickly set up to meet shortages, and I had to take the initiative to shape my work as a psychologist at the shelters myself. This required me to adapt quickly to diverse environments and to the various needs of the residents.

The emergency shelters where I worked varied tremendously in size. Some were small, accommodating only a few dozen residents; others were large enough to house hundreds of people. In all shelters, I collaborated closely with the staff in each shelter, including supervisors, general practitioners, and security personnel. The benefit of this collaboration was that they could keep a close eye on residents and inform me about those who were not feeling well and needed help.

Each of these shelters was like a village, a village populated by an extremely diverse group of people. Each of them had their own personalities, ideas, standards, and values. Some people displayed a positive outlook, while others tended to be more negative. There were those who quickly complained about one thing or another and others who were grateful for everything this country did for them. There were also moments of rebellion and conflict between residents. This is understandable given the diversity of nationalities, religious beliefs, and traumas that many have experienced. Added to this was the smallness of the living spaces that allowed little or no privacy. I try to imagine how my fellow compatriots and I would cope in such circumstances. I wonder about sharing a tiny unit with three women I have never met before and know nothing about–people with different day and night rhythms, not to mention that many have to deal with snoring roommates. (Using earplugs is not usually sufficient to deal with that!) I would struggle greatly in that situation; that's one thing I know for sure. It is actually quite impressive that a certain degree of peace was always maintained in the shelters where I worked.

In stark contrast with the conflicts, I have witnessed beautiful friendships develop and blossom. The shared experience of staying at the shelters provides a foundation upon which a strong bond can gradually develop among people. Everyone is in a similar situation; they have all fled and are all staying in a camp under similar circumstances. They know better than anyone outside how that feels. As the saying goes, "Shared sorrow is half the sorrow." When people had a transfer or when a shelter closed, I observed people saying goodbye to each other with hugs and tears in their eyes. As they parted, women said things like "Goodbye my sister!" These were women whose paths would probably never have crossed and therefore whose deep, heart-lifting connections would likely have never formed, without their time together in the shelter. I am convinced that the friendships and relationships that developed among these people will continue, wherever they may end up in the future.

The physical environment in which I myself worked reflected the challenges of the shelters themselves. Sometimes I was assigned a decent unit, but I also worked in small, impersonal units without windows where the bedding was also stored. In either case, my space was sometimes occupied with other important conversations taking place. In warm weather, I would sit outside with the people I was talking with in a place out of earshot.

I was allowed to use a telephone interpreter during conversations with clients but I rarely did. When dealing with sensitive psychological issues, most people prefer not to have a third person present. It creates a barrier, which is why I preferred using a translation app. Occasionally, a close friend whom my clients completely trusted would translate, providing a more comfortable alternative.

This meant that communication with people who didn't speak English mainly took place via a translation app. While this meant that conversations took more time and effort, it felt better for everyone. I quickly realized that it was essential to check what I said for accuracy, as the app didn't always translate correctly. The same applied to what the refugees communicated through the app. This sometimes resulted in hilarious translations. For instance, a man who was bothered by his roommates later told me, "I had a conversation with the vacuum cleaner, and after that, the problem was solved," as the translation app indicated. How wonderful it would be if everything could be resolved in this way! Moments like these provide us with laughter, which is essential.

At the shelters, I was more than just someone who conducted conversations from her office by appointment. It wasn't like I would say goodbye after a meeting with words like "See you next week!" I moved around the public hall, got my coffee or tea, and ate lunch in the dining room with the residents. This gave me the opportunity to engage in casual conversations, whether it was an update on their asylum application, a personal matter, or just a moment of relaxation, depending on their needs. These informal conversations added to my understanding and connection with them. The people were also interested in knowing how I was doing. These informal moments ensured that I was more than just a psychologist; I became a familiar face, and so the threshold for residents to approach me was lowered. At the small shelters, I knew everyone and everyone knew me. I knew how long they had been at the shelter, their backgrounds, and their concerns. Because I had regular contact with the residents, I felt involved in their situation and sympathized with them, both on a personal level and regarding their asylum applications.

Working at these shelters meant dealing with significant suffering and grief among the residents, alongside conflicts and challenging situations, which made working there quite demanding. However, working at the shelters wasn't only a place to provide care, it was also a place where I could experience humanity, warmth, and unexpected connections.

All these individuals had one thing in common: they were refugees seeking safety. With support from staff, they were able to achieve a degree of peace. We, as Christians, have one thing in common: we believe in Christ. How much should we be striving for peace and working towards building bridges?

How to Celebrate with Those Who Have Nothing

Rejoice with those who rejoice, weep with those who weep.
   Romans 12:15

As SEASONS CHANGE throughout the year, various holidays and celebrations come and go. Take the month of December, for instance. For many, besides celebrating the birth of Jesus, it is also a month that symbolizes time with family and friends, gifts, good food, drinks, and festive gatherings. December is often called the "party month," a month in which much is celebrated. But what does celebrating actually mean? When I hear the word "celebrate," I initially picture a party or a gathering full of joy where everyone seems happy and cheerful. But is that the only meaning of celebration?

For most people in the shelters, there is little to celebrate according to this definition. Joyful occasions are scarce, and many find themselves feeling anything but cheerful. This is not surprising; many are very uncertain about their future and are separated from loved ones they cannot see and deeply miss. Additionally, many have faced significant hardships in their home country and during the journey here. December is a month of joy for many. However, for those in shelters, it can be a time of reflection on their struggles. With so much difficulty behind them, there is not much to celebrate joyfully. Right?

Refugees lack the basic comforts that many of us take for granted: a place to call their own, furniture, work, and personal belongings. Their living conditions are basic, with a bed and food provided and a small allowance for essentials like shampoo and toothpaste. Beyond that, they have nothing, so to speak.

Who are the people at the shelters who seem to have nothing? Many have almost nothing in material terms and are uncertain about their future. Most face significant challenges and struggles in many ways—their whole lives have been turned upside down. Yet, what do I see in this group of people who seem to have nothing? A rock-solid, strong faith in God. They turn to God. That is the certainty and foundation that they DO have and to which they cling fiercely. I have seen this in most of them. Do I really want to keep saying that they have nothing?

What stands out to me about those who seem to have nothing is their mindset. As for the people I have supported, each of them had struggles and questions such as "what is the meaning of my life, when I can only sit here and wait for such a long time and do nothing?" or "why is my life so incredibly difficult?" However, I have never heard any of them blame God for their circumstances. What they did was bring their struggles honestly to God. They remained faithful to God, and their prayer life increased. Without exception, they all believe that God will one day bring justice for all the injustice that has been done to them.

What does it truly mean to celebrate in the face of hardship? I was deeply impressed and touched by a particular moment during my work. Sara was a Christian who, for many years, did not have access to a Bible and lacked the presence of fellow Christians. When she arrived in my country, all she had were the clothes she wore. By working hard at the shelter, she could afford a second-hand phone. I installed the Bible app for her, which also functioned in her native language. I opened the app, and her eyes widened to three times their usual size. The Bible that she had been able to carry only in her heart for so many years, she could finally read again. What a genuine moment to celebrate for both of us! A week later, she met with me again. For the first time, I saw her with a smile. Her first words were, "I have a bed, I have food, I have the Bible, and I even found a sister. I have everything." I will never forget that blissful look in her eyes. She had faith, hope, and love. Can I really believe that she had nothing?

Most people here have few or no possessions and are poor, which, of course, has a negative impact on their lives. However, the lack of material possessions and comfort doesn't mean that they have nothing, and it certainly doesn't mean they have nothing to celebrate. I create a safe space for them where they feel noticed and heard. I see them as fellow humans, and they know that I genuinely care for them. Isn't that something worth celebrating for those who often feel forgotten, unheard, and unnoticed? I see how small acts of kindness—a genuine smile or offering a listening ear—can transform a simple moment into something meaningful. This kind of connection brings comfort to those who need it most, but it also enriches my life.

Could I change the definition of celebration from "a joyful occasion where everyone seems to be happy and in a good mood" to "a special occasion where celebrating with those who have less can mean providing food, company, a listening ear, or just the feeling that they are valued and loved"? Could I adapt the so-called celebration to the occasion and the needs of the celebrant?

As I reflect on the meaning of celebration, I find myself thinking about Romans 12:15, where we are encouraged to "Rejoice with those who rejoice, and weep with those who weep." Those heart-stirring words intertwine beautifully with the wisdom found in James 1:27, which emphasizes the importance of caring for those who are in distress. Both of these messages resonate deeply with my experiences. Celebrating isn't just about joyful gatherings; it's also about recognizing the value of every individual and offering support to those in need. When I think back to that heartfelt moment of celebration with Sara, my heart still warms. This experience wasn't just about what I was able to give to Sara; I also received something valuable and precious.

Transformed by Compassion: My Journey Through Refugee Voices

And, apart from other things, there is the daily pressure on me of my anxiety for all the churches. Who is weak, and I am not weak? Who is made to fall, and I am not indignant?

— *2 Corinthians 11:28–29*

My own healing journey was the foundation for the empathy and strength I brought to my work with refugees, and I believe they recognized "my foundation." Many opened their hearts to me, sharing stories about their personal lives, families, cultures, and countries. I was with them in their pain but also in the joyful moments that were there as well. They showed me their thoughts and feelings and shared their hopes for a life in safety.

Working with refugees, hearing their stories, and understanding their reality opened my eyes and deepened my faith. I recall a woman I met at one of the shelters telling me, "I think it is an extraordinary experience for you right now. The work you are doing, getting to know people of different nationalities, fosters a huge amount of connection." She continued, "Just as talking to you reveals my point of view—my experiences and the pros and cons of my way of thinking, I am sure that talking to different people is a great plus for you to renew yourself and focus on your work and improve it." How true and well-said were these words from a refugee!

I have seen many people experience suffering, pain, and sadness. This has made me humble. It has helped me put things in perspective, especially the small issues in life where I would be worried or frustrated. Whenever I find myself doing this, I remind myself of their struggles. I ask myself, "How important is this that you are so worked up about it at all compared with their situation?" I have met people who have experienced significant loss and still count their blessings. People who, despite everything they have endured, continue to believe in the goodness of others. Despite all their struggles, they keep getting back up and continuing to go on, all in the hope of a life in safety. Their strength and courage command deep respect from me. It has taught me a lot.

Working with these individuals has required that I switch gears very quickly in response to the nationalities and variety of personal situations of each individual, whose issues could change any week. Sticking to a rigid plan for myself wouldn't work at all. For example, I would have a man share with me that his wife had to undergo a high-risk operation back home. Or someone would get a message from immigration about an upcoming interview. Situations like these cause high levels of stress for everyone concerned and create other needs. It is much more important to listen to these people and adjust to their needs than it is to follow through with a plan of action or treatment. This meant that I always had to take a wait-and-see approach to what each person needed and go from there. People don't always fit into a box, so being flexible and quick to adjust was essential.

People sometimes ask me: "How do you deal with all the misery you hear? I could never do that." Well, I do hear sad and terrible stories. Eventually, I "got used" to it and was no longer shocked by every story people shared, which to some extent can be seen as an advantage. It was important not to take over their emotions or get overly involved. That wouldn't be helpful for them, and it would exhaust and drain me. By familiarizing myself with what people experienced, I could offer them the support they needed. Of course, it was essential for me to process stories properly. What helped me was going out in nature and sharing thoughts with God. Even though I was "getting used" to the reality of things happening in the world, some stories still left me silent and shocked after my workday. Once, a young woman told me that she and her husband weren't allowed to laugh. She had to live with her in-laws, who held the belief that laughing was sinful. Anything involving a smile or laughter was punished by severe abuse. Imagine not being permitted to smile, and if you did, getting punished for that! How often have you laughed and smiled this week?

I now have an enhanced appreciation for Paul's heart for his brethren per 2 Corinthians 11:28–29. All his physical trials were small compared to his deep concern for all the churches. There's a cost to caring, but caring's worth that cost. I chose to bear that cost by helping refugees; the cost was stout, but it continues to bless me. It will continue to bless me all of my days.

Had I known the costs and frustrations in advance, would I still have leaned into helping refugees? Yes, a thousand times over. Choosing to care, listen, and help even within major limitations has invited God to make me better. I love Him more. I'm more aware of His grace. And I know helping others is a crucial part of my heart.

This world is not a kind place, and it probably never will be. A tremendous amount of abuse and violence takes place in the world. Terrible, unbelievable things are happening to people. I will never really get used to that, but I cannot change what happens in the world. What I can do is to be there for the people who need me and make them feel seen and heard. Though this may not seem like much, for them it can make a huge difference! Furthermore, hearing their personal stories allowed me to understand the depth of their pain and hardship. This truly opened my heart, and I developed a deep compassion for what they had been through. Now I genuinely understand why God gave us the commandment in the Bible to care for the stranger. Now I see why the stranger is mentioned together with the widow and the orphan, and why they were also specially protected by God.

Closing my own door in 2019 resulted in various losses for me, some of which were unexpected. Those unexpected hurts were the ones that hit me the hardest. Being on a journey of healing myself, I experienced the importance of a support system and community. I was truly blessed to receive support from my friends as well as from my church family. This made me become even more aware of the importance of community. We don't know what life will bring us or where it will take us, but having a community is an essential factor—and a reminder that we all need to keep going, especially when times are tough. I recognize that there are people who are utterly alone in this country, and I understand what it means to them to be seen, heard, and included by others.

But before I could truly change my perspective on refugees and the world, I first needed to change "where I was." That meant stepping out of my usual setting, experiences, and even my comfort zone in order to gain this new outlook. I literally needed to be immersed "in their world," so to speak, to gain this understanding of and compassion for them. Many nationalities, many worlds. It was only when I entered their worlds—and "changed where I was"—that I could change my perspective. I can only present this experience as an enormous enrichment and blessing. It was a tremendous privilege to walk a part of the journey with this group of people who have been through so much.

As I conclude this record about my journey through the lives and stories of refugees, I am reminded that each one of them carries a unique story—one of pain but also one of hope and resilience. It takes a lot to leave your home country and the people who are near and dear to you. It is not easy to be here as a refugee; "not easy" is quite an understatement! I see the vulnerability of these people who leave everything familiar in search of safety; I now understand better the struggles and challenges they face. Their voices have not only shaped my understanding of the world but also inspired me to start writing—writing to speak up for those who are often unheard.

From Inspiration to Impact

If you feel inspired after reading this book, there are several ways to make a difference:

- Make a Financial Contribution: Donate money to local, national, or international refugee organizations. It is a straightforward way to make a difference. Every amount, big or small, helps fund crucial programs and services.
- Volunteer: Get involved with local, national, or international organizations that support refugees. This could include offering language classes, job training, or mentorship. Many also provide remote volunteering opportunities.
- Raise Awareness and Advocate for Refugees: Share articles, stories, and

personal experiences about refugees on social media to encourage compassion and combat misinformation.

Whether you have resources, time, or simply a desire to raise awareness, every action counts in making a positive impact.

For more information, visit threadsofruth.org.

Also by Cypress Publications

I AM: A Study of the. True and Living God edited by Jeremy Barrier and Charles R. Webb

Jesus the Christ: Chapters for Bible Teachers by Ed Gallagher

Supporting Sisters: A Biblical Approach to Helping One Another Through Life's Struggles by Kim Chalmers

WHAM! Facing Life's Heavy Hits: Thirteen New Testament Encounters by Bill Bagents and Laura S. Bagents

WHAM! Facing Life's Heavy Hits: Thirteen Old Testament Encounters by Bill Bagents and Laura S. Bagents

To see a full catalog of Heritage Christian University
Press and its imprint Cypress Publications, visit
www.hcu.edu/publications

www.ingramcontent.com/pod-product-compliance
Lightning Source LLC
Chambersburg PA
CBHW020554030426
42337CB00013B/1100